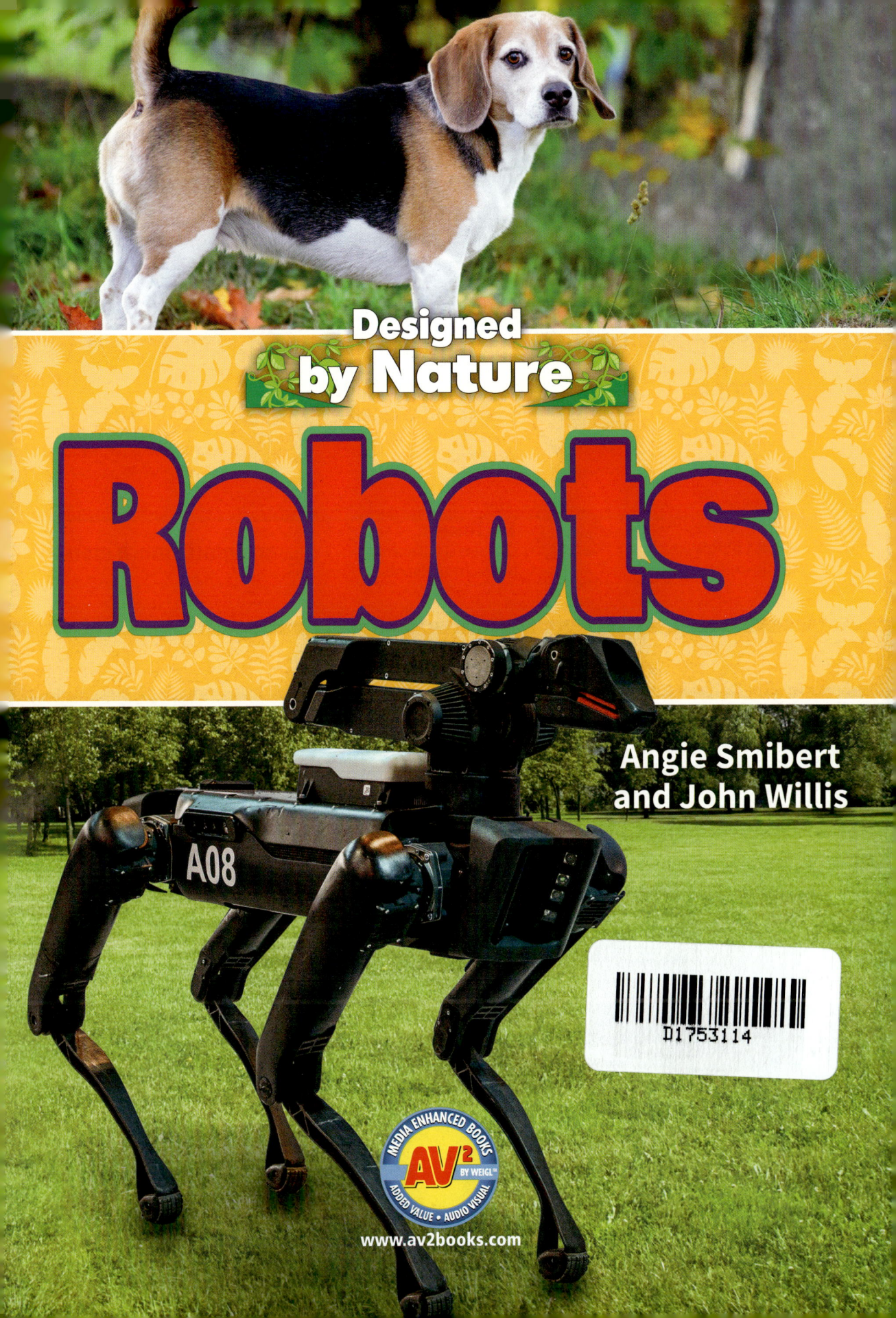
Robots

Designed by Nature

Angie Smibert and John Willis

www.av2books.com

AV² provides enriched content that supplements and complements this book. Weigl's AV² books strive to create inspired learning and engage young minds in a total learning experience.

Your AV² Media Enhanced books come alive with...

 **Audio** Listen to sections of the book read aloud.

 **Key Words** Study vocabulary, and complete a matching word activity.

 **Video** Watch informative video clips.

 **Quizzes** Test your knowledge.

 **Embedded Weblinks** Gain additional information for research.

 **Slide Show** View images and captions, and prepare a presentation.

 **Try This!** Complete activities and hands-on experiments.

Go to www.av2books.com, and enter this book's unique code.

BOOK CODE

AVD26563

AV² by Weigl brings you media enhanced books that support active learning.

... and much, much more!

Published by AV² by Weigl
350 5th Avenue, 59th Floor
New York, NY 10118
Website: www.av2books.com

Copyright © 2020 AV² by Weigl
All rights reserved. No part of this publication may be reproduced, stored in a retrieval system, or transmitted in any form or by any means, electronic, mechanical, photocopying, recording, or otherwise, without the prior written permission of the publisher.

Library of Congress Cataloging-in-Publication Data available upon request.
Fax 1-866-44-WEIGL for the attention of the Publishing Records department.

ISBN 978-1-4896-9729-5 (hardcover)
ISBN 978-1-4896-9730-1 (softcover)
ISBN 978-1-4896-9731-8 (multi-user eBook)
ISBN 978-1-4896-9732-5 (single-user eBook)

Printed in the United States of America in Brainerd, Minnesota
1 2 3 4 5 6 7 8 9 0   22 21 20 19 18

122018
102318

Project Coordinator: John Willis   Designer: Ana María Vidal

Every reasonable effort has been made to trace ownership and to obtain permission to reprint copyright material. The publishers would be pleased to have any errors or omissions brought to their attention so that they may be corrected in subsequent printings.

Weigl acknowledges Alamy, Dreamstime, Getty Images, iStock, Shutterstock, and Wikimedia as its primary image suppliers for this title.

First published by North Star Editions in 2019

Designed by Nature

Contents

AV² Book Code 2

CHAPTER 1
Bots That Bend 4

CHAPTER 2
Bots That Swim 10

INSPIRE ME!
Swimming in Venice 15

CHAPTER 3
Bots That Fly 16

CHAPTER 4
Bots of the Future 22

Timeline 27

Robotics Map 28

Quiz 30

Key Words 31

Index 31

Log on to
www.av2books.com 32

Robots 3

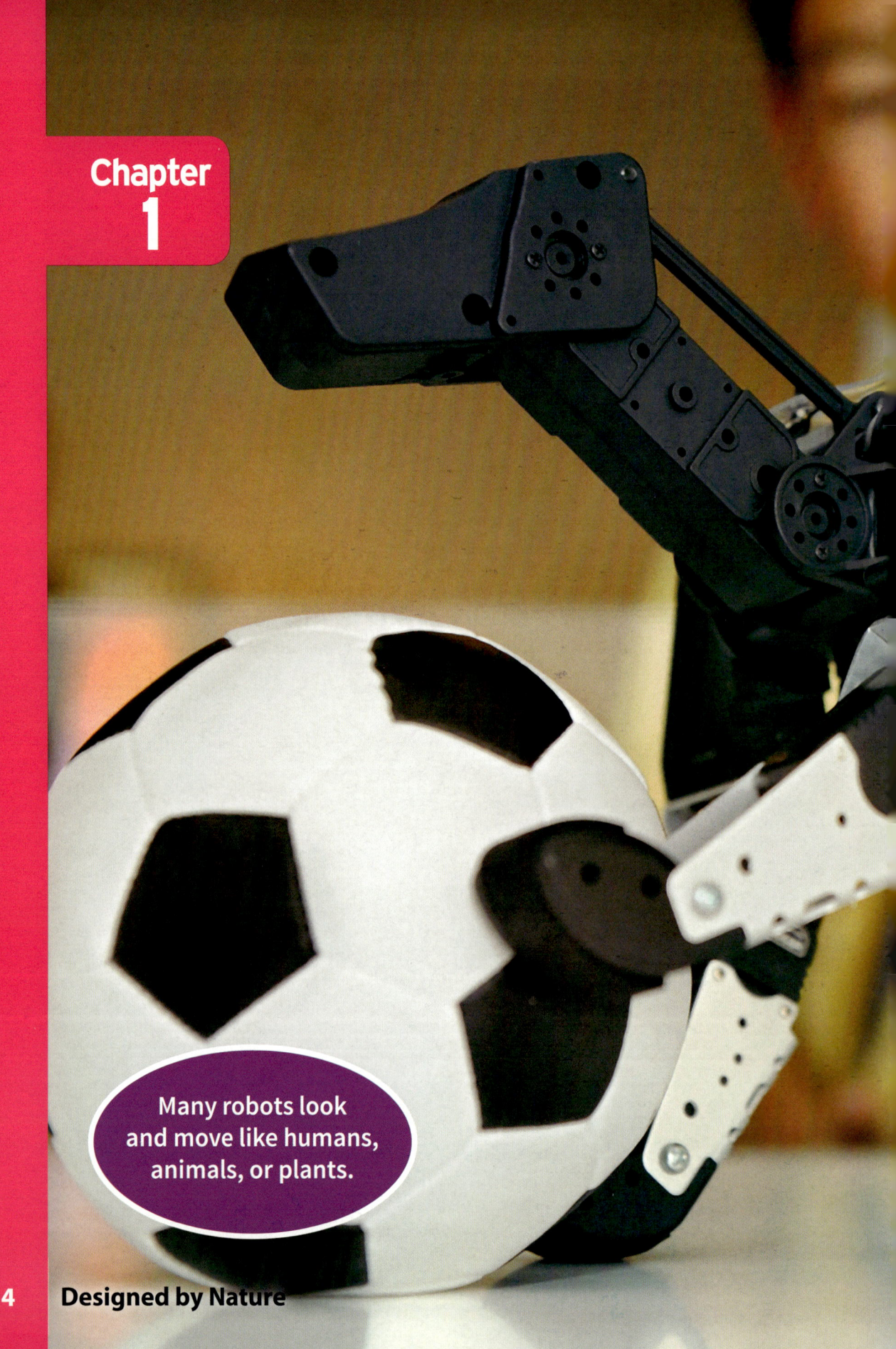

Chapter 1

Many robots look and move like humans, animals, or plants.

Designed by Nature

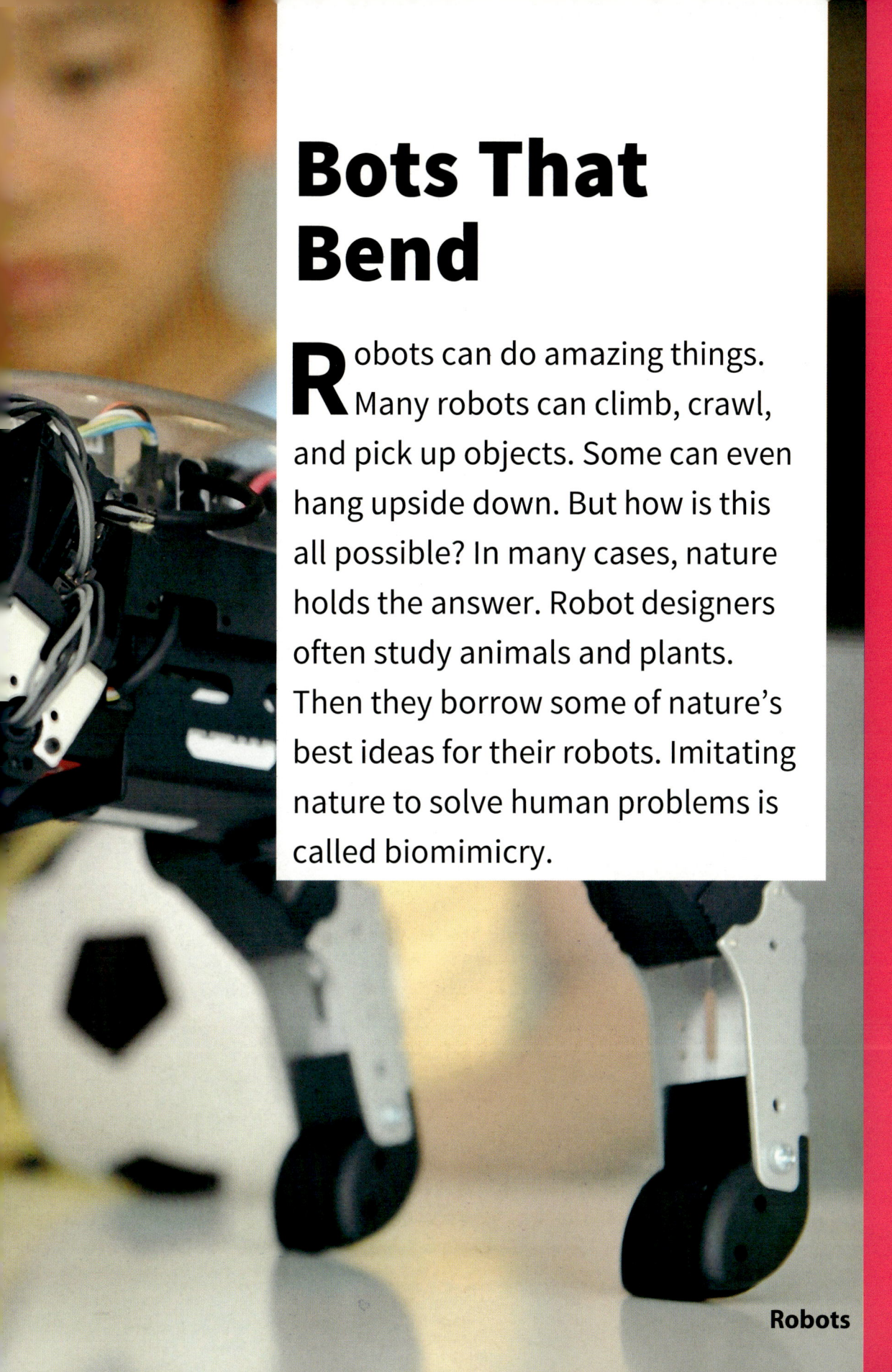

Bots That Bend

Robots can do amazing things. Many robots can climb, crawl, and pick up objects. Some can even hang upside down. But how is this all possible? In many cases, nature holds the answer. Robot designers often study animals and plants. Then they borrow some of nature's best ideas for their robots. Imitating nature to solve human problems is called biomimicry.

Inspired by Vines

English ivy is a vine that grows and spreads quickly. Researchers have built a robot that moves like this plant does. The robot's body is a long, flexible tube. The tube expands to become longer. Then it curls around objects like a growing vine. The bot can even go under doors, through cracks, and around corners.

English ivy grows slowly for its first two years. By its third year, it grows very quickly.

For instance, one group of scientists studied the way snakes move. In 2008, they created Snakebot. This robot has 16 motors along its body. When the motors move, Snakebot crawls across the floor. Snakebot can also wrap around a person's leg. The robot can be used for **search and rescue**. The same scientists also invented HARP. This robot looks like a snake, too. But it is designed to help with heart surgery.

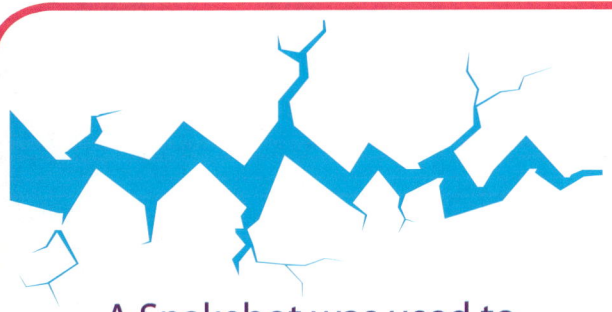

A Snakebot was used to help search for survivors after a magnitude **7.1 earthquake** in Mexico in 2017.

The snakebot used in Mexico was **3 feet long**. (0.9 meters)

Snakebot was named the 2017 Ground Rescue **Robot of the Year**.

Other scientists created the Bionic Handling Assistant in 2010. This robotic arm is similar to an elephant's trunk. It has three flexible **segments**. These segments allow the arm to bend. The end of the arm has gripper fingers. They can bend and wrap around objects, much like an elephant's trunk can.

Other animals have inspired robots that can move and grip. Some robots can run like cheetahs. Others can climb walls like geckos. In 2015, scientists released a robot called Spot. The robot's legs can bend and move like a dog's. Spot can run and walk over snow, ice, mud, and rough terrain. It can climb better than many vehicles. The US Marines have been testing Spot to use with soldiers. One day, robots such as these might deliver packages or rescue people in danger.

US Marines may someday use Spot during missions.

Chapter 2

Although related to snails, octopuses do not have shells. The only hard parts of their bodies are their beaks.

Bots That Swim

Robot designers often turn to the ocean for ideas. Some robots **mimic** the way sea creatures swim and communicate. Other robots may look or feel like sea creatures. Many underwater animals have soft bodies. These animals have inspired scientists to make soft robots.

Most robots require hard materials such as metal. But soft robots are made of flexible materials. Without hard parts, they are safer for human use.

One example of a soft robot is known as Octobot. This robot moves like an octopus does. Octopuses do not have skeletons. Yet they are incredibly strong. They use their arms to grip and swim. Octobot does this, too.

Octobot has no wires or metal parts. Instead, it uses gas to move its tentacles. The robot turns a small amount of liquid fuel into gas. This gas flows through the robot's arms. The gas inflates the actuators in the arms. An actuator is the part that makes a machine move. When Octobot's actuators inflate, its arms flex. This allows the robot to swim. It is the first soft robot that moves on its own.

OctopusGripper, another robot based on an octopus, uses suction cups to help hold objects.

Octobot

Octobot is made of soft parts that work together.

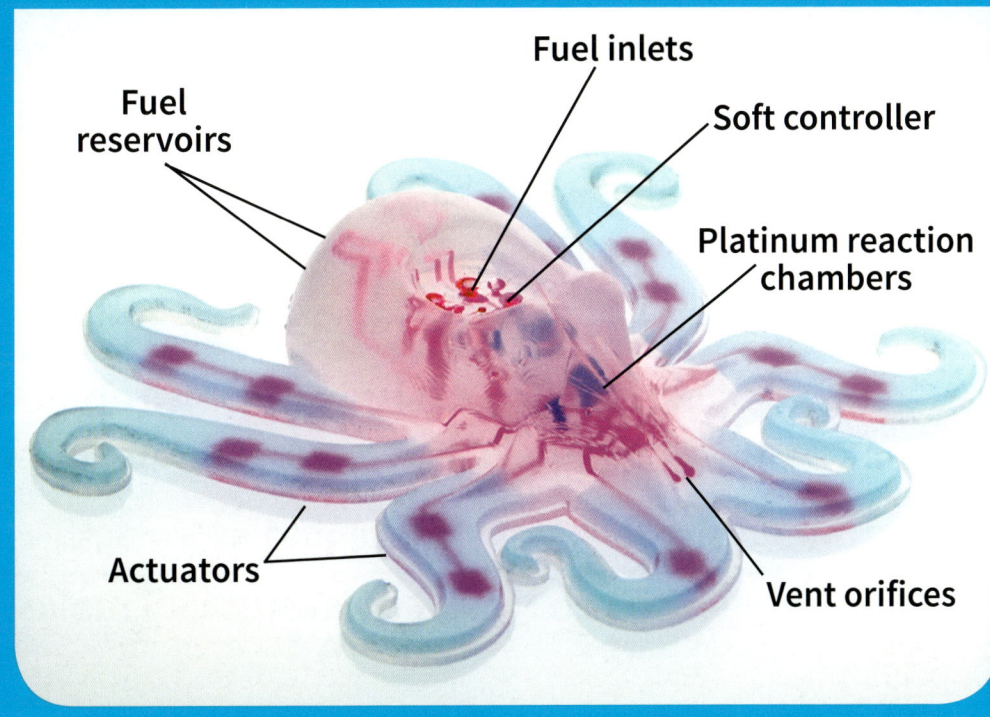

Fuel inlets
Fuel reservoirs
Soft controller
Platinum reaction chambers
Actuators
Vent orifices

Many hard robots are based on sea creatures, too. For instance, Robojelly is a robot that looks and moves like a moon jellyfish. This animal moves by flexing muscles around its body. The body folds in like a closing umbrella. This forces water out and pushes the animal forward.

To move like a jellyfish, a robot's body must bend and fold. So, designers covered Robojelly with a thick layer of **silicone**. Instead of muscles, the robot has thin wires made of a flexible metal. The metal can bend and then return to its original shape. These materials allow Robojelly to fold and unfold. The robot pushes out water to move like a jellyfish.

Robojelly could be used for underwater search and rescue. It could also be used to study the environment. Robojelly may even be able to clean up oil spills. In the future, robots will work more and more with humans. Robots inspired by sea creatures will make this possible.

Moon jellyfish change color based on their diet. Jellyfish that eat crustaceans turn pinkish.

Designed by Nature

Inspire Me!

Swimming in Venice

The city of Venice, Italy, sits on the Venetian Lagoon. In 2017, the lagoon became home to robots. The aPad floats on the water's surface, similar to a lily pad. The aMussel sits on the seabed. And the aFish swims in shallow water. These robots work together to collect data.

To navigate, the aFish and aMussel use an electric sense. Their inventors were inspired by the elephant fish. This fish has organs that create an **electric field**. The fish can sense when an object enters this field. The robots in Venice work in a similar way. They use built-in sensors to find their way around.

The Venetian Lagoon is in danger of flooding and pollution. Scientists hope the robots will teach them more about the lagoon. Then, humans can do more to protect it.

Eventually, scientists plan to have 120 robots in the Venetian Lagoon.

Chapter 3

SmartBird's design was based on a herring gull.

Bots That Fly

The ability to fly has fascinated humans for centuries. Scientists studied birds to build the first airplanes. Now, robot designers are also studying birds. Scientists built SmartBird in 2011. This robot has wings that beat up and down, similar to the wings of a bird. As the robot flies, it can twist its body, wings, and tail. That way, it can turn or fly higher. As the robot's wings flap up, they angle upward to create lift. This mimics the actions of a bird.

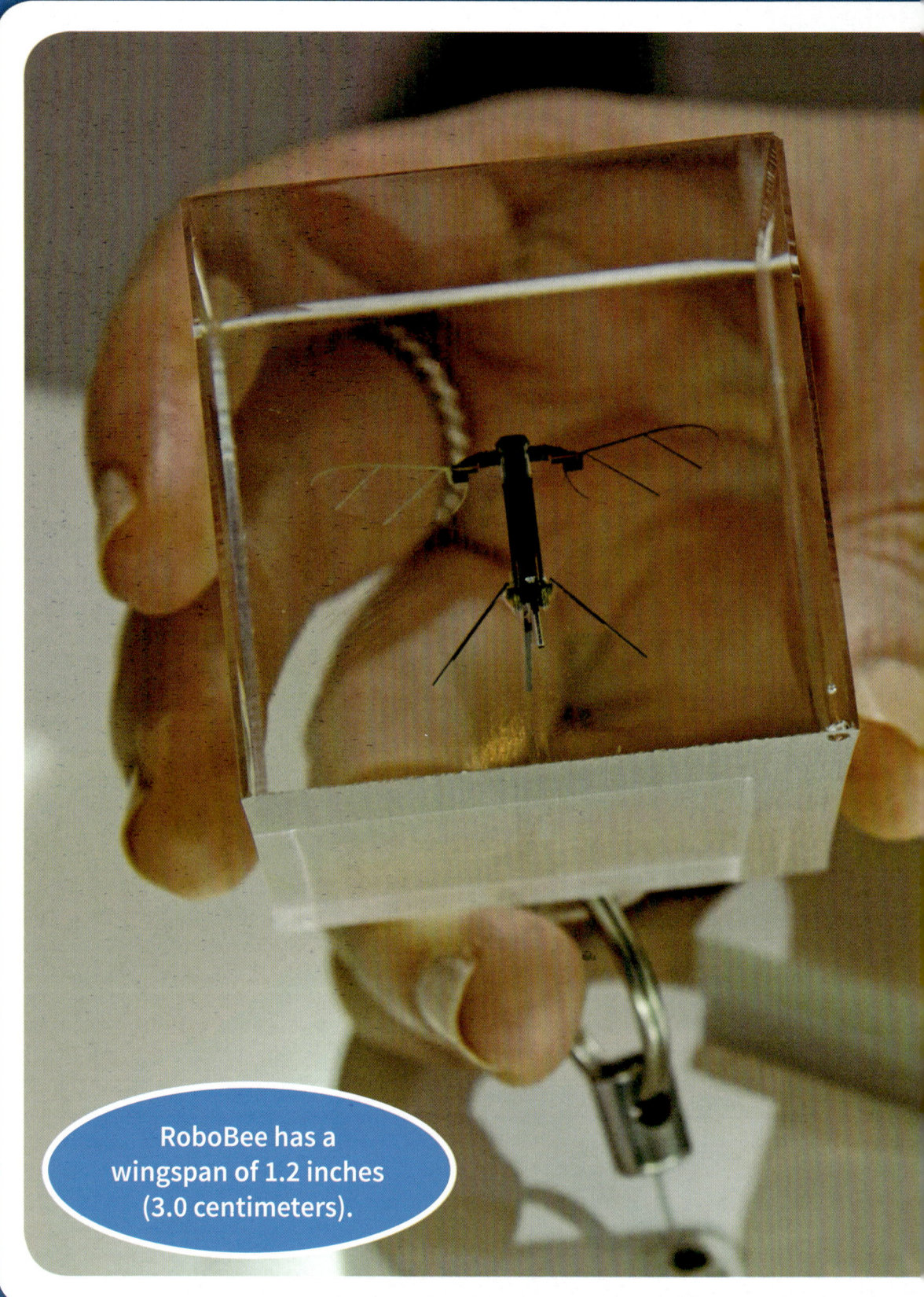

RoboBee has a wingspan of 1.2 inches (3.0 centimeters).

Insects have also inspired robots. For instance, the tiny RoboBee can lift, hover, and fly. The first model was smaller than a paperclip. Newer models of RoboBee can land and stick to surfaces. They can even swim. But a RoboBee is too small to break the surface of water. Instead, it hovers over water and turns off its wings. Then it falls into the water at an angle. The robot's dive was inspired by the puffin. This small seabird also dives into water at an angle. To swim, RoboBee flaps its wings nine times per second.

Some robots can fly in a group, similar to a **swarm** of insects. Robots known as eMotionButterflies can fly by flapping their ultralight wings. These robots can fly on their own or as a swarm. Designers use a computer program to guide them.

Designers can tell the robots how to behave. For instance, one robot might have to stay a certain distance from another robot. After giving these commands, no one needs to guide the robots. The robots use **infrared** sensors and an indoor **GPS** system. These tools prevent them from flying into objects.

By studying nature, scientists have found new ways to make robots fly. In the future, swarm robotics could have many uses. For example, robot swarms could be used for search and rescue. They could also clean up the environment. The sky is the limit!

Swarm Robotics

Many insects are social. Together, they can perform amazing tasks, such as building a hive. This ability is called swarm intelligence. Swarm robotics mimics this ability in robots. Individual robots are given simple commands. But all the robots work together. As a group, they can perform complex tasks.

Swarm robotics could allow robots to mimic the flying formation of birds.

Chapter 4

Octopuses use camouflage both to hide from predators and to catch prey.

Bots of the Future

It can take years for scientists to design, create, and test robots. Many robots are still in their early stages. And many robot designers are looking for new ideas. Some are studying how animals perform specific behaviors.

Camouflage is one of the behaviors that robot designers are interested in. Camouflage allows some animals to hide in plain sight. For instance, an octopus can change the color and texture of its skin. This allows the animal to blend in with its surroundings.

Nanobots

Nanobots are even smaller than microbots. However, very few nanobots exist. In 2016, British scientists won the Nobel Prize. They built the first nanobot made out of molecules. A molecule is a group of atoms bonded together. It is the smallest unit of a substance that has all the parts of that substance. The scientists' nanobot is very small. One strand of hair is 1,000 times as wide as their nanobot.

Events such as the Consumer Electronics Show (CES) allow companies to showcase new developments in fields such as robotics.

Scientists have made **artificial** octopus skin. This material can change color. And its texture can change from flat to bumpy. Scientists hope to use the artificial skin on soft robots. The skin would help the robots hide in nature. Some scientists use robots to observe animals in the wild. Camouflage would protect the robots from being attacked or eaten.

Other robot designers want to recreate features of the world's tiniest creatures. Microbots are very tiny robots. Some are the size of a fly. Others are small enough to swim in a human's bloodstream. These microbots could be useful in medicine. For example, microbots might help fight cancer. They could carry drugs toward tumors in the body.

A team of six **1.1-inch** (2.8-cm) long microbots was used to slowly tow a car.

Robobees flap their wings **120 times** each second.

The world's **smallest moving**, untethered robot is only one tenth as thick as human hair.

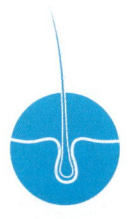

A new microbot design mimics the paramecium. The paramecium is a tiny organism covered in hairs called cilia. The cilia move back and forth to help the creature move. Designers are now testing cilia on microbots. Microbots with cilia move up to 25 times faster than microbots without them. This could help microbots reach cancer cells very quickly.

Nature will always inspire robots. Answers from plants and animals have solved many of the problems robot designers face. And many new ideas are yet to be discovered.

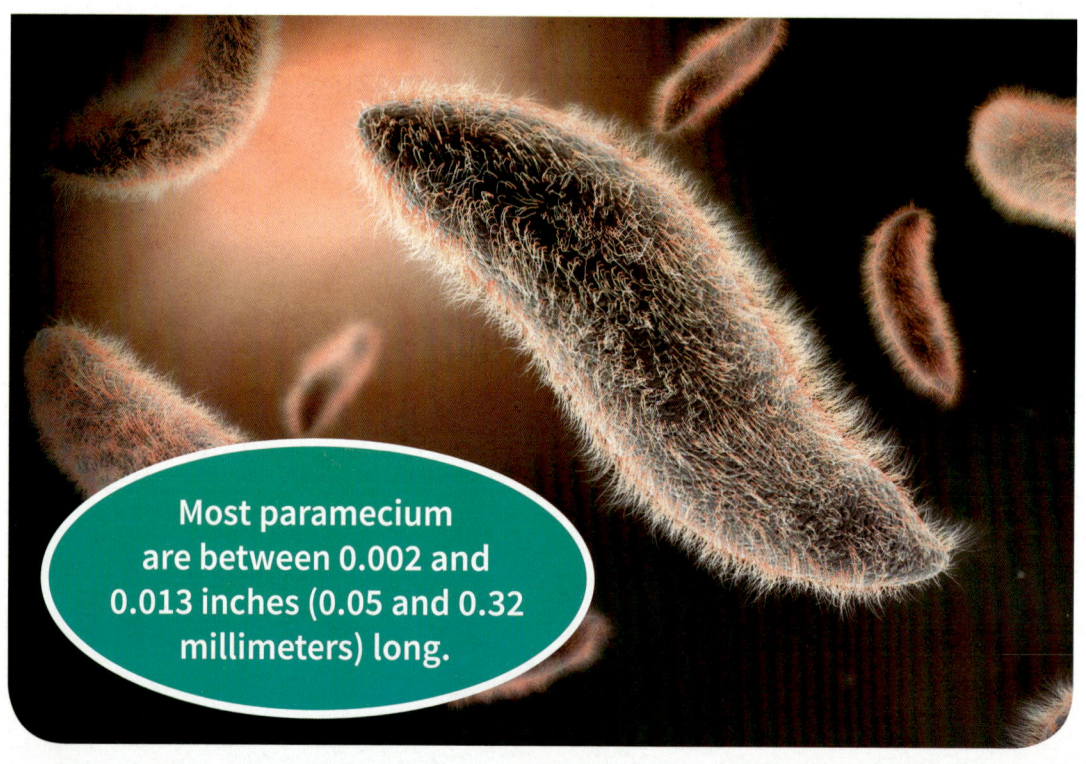

Most paramecium are between 0.002 and 0.013 inches (0.05 and 0.32 millimeters) long.

Timeline

The word "robot" was first introduced in the 20th century. Since then, people have turned to nature to create robots for a wide variety of different tasks.

2011 An Italian engineering team develops robot arms based on octopus limbs.

2012 Engineers at the University of Virginia develop a swimming robot based on the movement of rays.

2015 Robotics company Boston Dynamics reveals Spot, a robot dog that can climb stairs and move through rough terrain.

2016 Robirds are first used at airports. These robots, shaped like birds of prey, are used to scare away other birds to keep aircraft safe.

2017 An engineering team at the Georgia Institute of Technology develops Tarzan the Robot, a crop monitoring robot with movement based on a sloth.

2018 HAMR-F, a cockroach-based robot built by Harvard engineers, is developed. It has an onboard battery and can move at a speed of four body lengths per second.

Robotics Map

Robotics companies and engineers around the world have turned to nature for inspiration when looking for the answers to many questions. Today, more and more nature-based designs are being used for many different purposes.

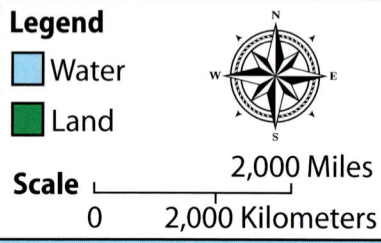

Legend
- Water
- Land

Scale: 2,000 Miles / 2,000 Kilometers

United States
Boston Dynamics is well known for its advances in biomimetic technology. The company has made a wide range of different robots that can complete tasks ranging from sprinting to doing backflips.

Great Britain
In 2016, LaserSnake2, a large snake-shaped robot, was used to help decommission a power cell in Sellafield, Great Britain. The robot, equipped with a powerful laser, is used to cut apart objects.

Designed by Nature

Italy
At the Sant'Anna School of Advanced Studies in Pisa, Italy, Professor Cecilia Laschi developed an octopus-inspired robot. In addition to its flexible legs, it could draw in and expel water to move like an octopus would in nature.

Japan
Researchers at Keio University and the University of Tokyo created a 32-legged robot called Mochibot. Based on a sea urchin, it is able to move over a wide range of terrain.

Quiz

1 When does English ivy begin growing quickly?
Answer: After three years

2 What was RoboBee's dive based on?
Answer: A puffin

3 What are the hairs on a paramecium called?
Answer: Cilia

4 What robot was created by researchers at Keio University and the University of Tokyo?
Answer: Mochibot

5 When was the first nanobot built?
Answer: 2016

6 What is swarm intelligence?
Answer: The ability of groups of insects to perform complex tasks

7 What city is on the Venetian Lagoon in Italy?
Answer: Venice

8 What kind of robot was used to search for survivors after a 2017 earthquake in Mexico?
Answer: A snakebot

9 What bird was SmartBird's design based on?
Answer: A herring gull

10 What does Octobot use to move its tentacles?
Answer: Gas

Designed by Nature

Key Words

artificial: made by humans instead of occurring naturally

camouflage: a pattern that is designed to look like its surroundings

electric field: a force that surrounds an electric charge or group of charges

GPS: a navigation system that uses satellites to figure out location.

infrared: light that is invisible to human eyes but can be seen by certain cameras

mimic: to copy an appearance or behavior

search and rescue: the activity of finding and helping people in danger

segments: different parts that make up a body or object

silicone: a tough, human-made substance made from the chemical element silicon

swarm: a large number of insects moving together

Index

aFish 15
aMussel 15
aPad 15

Bionic Handling Assistant 8

camouflage 22, 23, 25

eMotionButterflies 19
English ivy 6, 30

HARP 7
herring gull 16, 30

microbots 24, 25, 26

nanobots 24, 30

Octobot 11, 12, 13, 30

paramecium 26, 30
puffin 19, 30

RoboBee 18, 19, 25, 30
Robojelly 13, 14

search and rescue 7, 14, 20
SmartBird 16, 17, 30
Snakebot 7, 30
soft robotics 11, 12, 25
Spot 8, 9, 27
swarm robotics 19, 20, 21, 30

US Marines 8, 9

Venetian Lagoon 15, 30

Log on to www.av2books.com

AV² by Weigl brings you media enhanced books that support active learning. Go to www.av2books.com, and enter the special code found on page 2 of this book. You will gain access to enriched and enhanced content that supplements and complements this book. Content includes video, audio, weblinks, quizzes, a slide show, and activities.

AV² Online Navigation

Audio
Listen to sections of the book read aloud

Book Pages
AV² pages directly correspond to pages in the book.

Video
Watch informative video clips.

Embedded Weblinks
Gain additional information for research.

Key Words
Study vocabulary, and complete a matching word activity.

Try This!
Complete activities and hands-on experiments.

Quizzes
Test your knowledge.

Slide Show
View images and captions, and prepare a presentation.

AV² was built to bridge the gap between print and digital. We encourage you to tell us what you like and what you want to see in the future.

Sign up to be an AV² Ambassador at www.av2books.com/ambassador.

Due to the dynamic nature of the Internet, some of the URLs and activities provided as part of AV² by Weigl may have changed or ceased to exist. AV² by Weigl accepts no responsibility for any such changes. All media enhanced books are regularly monitored to update addresses and sites in a timely manner. Contact AV² by Weigl at 1-866-649-3445 or av2books@weigl.com with any questions, comments, or feedback.